Contents

Some words are printed in bold, **like this**. You can find out what they mean in the glossary. You can also look in the box at the bottom of the page where the word first appears.

STARTING OUT

To some people, skateboarding is more than just a hobby. It is a way of life.

Skaters begin by learning fairly simple moves, such as how to **tic-tac**. Then, they try harder moves such as **grinds** and **slides**.

Getting to know the board

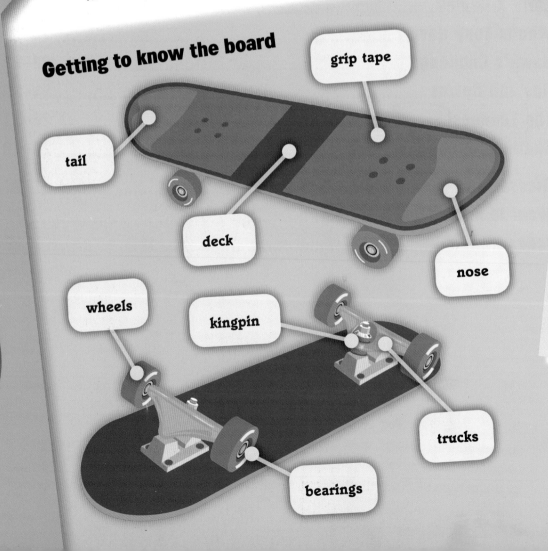

grip tape

tail

deck

nose

wheels

kingpin

trucks

bearings

Skateboarders spend hours on their boards.

grind	move in which a skater slides the truck (bar that is between the wheels) of a skateboard along a surface
slide	move in which a skater skids the middle of a skateboard against a surface
tic-tac	move in which a skater pushes down on the back and front of a board to move without a foot pushing off the ground

The boy on the right
is doing an ollie.

STREET SKATING

Skaters like to perform a lot of moves. One move is called an ollie. This is when skaters leap in the air and make their boards rise up with them.

Where do skaters practise?

Performing moves such as ollies and jumps is called **street skating**. Skaters practise these moves on pavements or in **skate parks**.

Extreme fact!

When skaters get very good at doing ollies, they can jump over kerbs, rails, and park benches.

skate park	area that has been set aside just for skaters
street skating	using the surfaces in a street to do tricks such as jumps and grinds

WHAT IS NEXT?

Once they can do street moves, many skaters try the ramps.

Tricks in the air

Skaters who perform on ramps are called **vert skaters**. This is because so much of their action is vertical (up and down).

On a **halfpipe**, skaters build up speed. They can do spins, twists, and **grabs** in the air. Then they come back down onto the ramp.

A skater **grinds** on the coping of a halfpipe ramp.

grab	move in which the skater reaches down and touches part of the skateboard while skating
halfpipe	large, curved, up-and-down ramp that skaters use to go up in the air

transition

flat

coping

deck

vert skating

skating that involves vertical movement, such as on a halfpipe

How Skating Began

Skateboarding started in the 1960s in California, United States. It began because there were many surfers in California who used skateboards to practise surfing moves on pavements.

The skating story

In the 1970s, a lot of **skate parks** were built in many Californian cities. Skaters used the ramps and **bowls** in the parks. As skating became more popular, skaters started competing more seriously.

Extreme fact!

One of the first skate parks to open in the UK was in Portobello, London in 1976.

bowl   cement or wooden skate park area shaped like a cereal bowl

A skater does a kickflip over an obstacle at a skate park.

These skaters are filming each other.

GOING PRO

Some people get so good at skateboarding that they can earn a lot of money.

Practice makes perfect

Most professional (pro) skaters live near **skate parks**. Others have **halfpipes** in their gardens. To win competition prize money, they may need to practise for hours each day.

Many skaters ask friends to film them as they practise. They later watch the film and study their moves.

Extreme fact!

Skateboarding is the top extreme sport among teenage boys. It is more popular than BMX racing or motocross.

motocross   type of motorcycle racing on dirt tracks

GET READY TO SKATE

Before skating, pros do stretches and warm-up moves. Many of the muscles used to ride a skateboard are not the same ones used in everyday life.

What do skaters wear?

Skaters take care of their bodies by wearing safety helmets. **Vert skaters** wear elbow pads and knee pads. If they fall on the ramp, the pads will protect them.

Extreme fact!

Pro skaters do not try new moves without planning them first.

Safety gear is an important part of skating.

Skaters do moves high
above the crowds.

SKATING INJURIES

Injuries will always be a part of skateboarding. Many injuries happen when skateboarders try doing tricks on halfpipes.

Dangerous halfpipes

Halfpipes are very tall, usually between 2.4 and 3.7 metres (8 and 12 feet) high. The halfpipes at competitions can be bigger. If a skater falls from this height, it may cause injury.

Skaters take turns on ramps. When more than one skater is in a halfpipe, there is more chance for injury. A mid-air crash between skaters would be very dangerous.

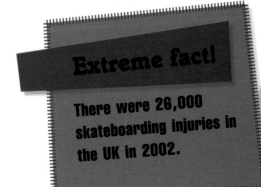

Extreme fact!

There were 26,000 skateboarding injuries in the UK in 2002.

EARLY X-GAMES

In 1995, the **X-Games** became the first major extreme sports competition.

How important are the X-Games?

The X-Games have become the most popular skating competition in the world. Pro skaters work all year to take part in the X-Games. The games have grown to become a worldwide event.

X-Games   **worldwide action sports competition**

The X-Games started in 1995
as the Extreme Games.

Tony Hawk has won a lot of X-Games medals.

WHO IS TONY HAWK?

Tony Hawk won local contests in California, United States when he was only 12 years old. By the time he was 17, he had bought his own house with prize money.

The best yet

Hawk has 16 **X-Games** medals. He has won medals for **vert skating**, **street skating**, best trick, and **vert doubles**. From 1997 to 2002, Hawk and skater Andy MacDonald won gold medals in vert doubles every year.

Extreme fact!

Hawk got his first skateboard in 1977. It was a ninth birthday gift from his brother. Hawk is still a top skater today.

vert doubles contest where a team of two skaters performs on a vert ramp at the same time

HAWK'S CHALLENGE

The 900 is one of the most difficult moves in vert skating, because the skater must turn two-and-a-half times in the air.

Giving it another spin

At the 1999 **X-Games**, Tony Hawk became the first skater to land a 900 in a competition. However, he landed after his time ran out. It did not count.

At the 2003 X–Games, Hawk tried the 900 again. This time, he finished the trick during the contest. He won the "best trick" competition easily.

Hawk tried to land the 900 for ten years. He was finally able to do it in public.

Jumping out of a helicopter is one of Danny Way's tricks. He zooms onto the halfpipe and makes a huge jump above the other deck.

Ups and Downs

Spins are moves where the skater changes direction in the air instead of landing on the deck. The best skaters also get amazing height.

Who has the world record?

In 1999, skater Danny Way set the world record for highest spin during a trick. He soared 5 metres (16.5 feet) above a ramp. The halfpipe was 5.5 metres (18 feet) tall.

Extreme fact!

Danny Way dropped out of a helicopter onto a ramp to attempt tricks.

THE YOUNGEST

One of the hottest skaters today is Ryan Sheckler.

Can the youngest win the X-Games?

In 2003, Sheckler became the youngest ever winner of an **X-Games** gold medal. He was only 13 years old. He showed off his **street skating** skills in the **skate park** contest.

Extreme fact!

Sheckler once went to a doctor because he broke his right arm skating. The doctor told him that his left elbow was also broken. Sheckler did not even know it!

Sheckler still spends more than 20 hours each week skating. He works hard on his moves.

Shaun White is a true double threat. He is a pro skateboader and snowboarder!

take-off

landing ramp

Danny Way jumped over the 19.5 metre (64-foot) wide Great Wall of China.

SKATING'S FUTURE

Some pro skaters have turned skateboarding into a lifelong career. Skaters continue to set more amazing records all the time.

start

A name to watch out for

Shaun White is the first athlete to win the Summer and Winter **X-Games**. He has won in both skateboarding and snowboarding. White won the Olympic gold medal for snowboarding in 2006. He was just 19 years old.

Extreme fact!

Gary Hardwick is the fastest man on a board. In 1998, he hit 100 km (63 miles) per hour.

Glossary

bowl cement or wooden skate park area shaped like a cereal bowl

grab move in which the skater reaches down and touches part of the skateboard while skating

grind move in which a skater slides the truck (bar that is between the wheels) of a skateboard along a surface

halfpipe large, up-and-down ramp that skaters use to go up in the air

motocross type of motorcycle racing on dirt tracks

skate park area that has been set aside just for skaters

slide move in which a skater skids the middle of a skateboard against a surface

street skating using the surfaces in a street to do tricks such as jumps and grinds

tic-tac move in which a skater pushes down on the back and front of a board to move without a foot pushing off the ground

vert doubles contest where a team of two skaters performs on a vert ramp at the same time

vert skating skating that involves vertical movement, such as on a halfpipe

X-Games worldwide action sports competition

Want to Know More?

Books

✳ *Radical Sports: Skateboarding*, Andy Horsley (Heinemann Library, 2002)

✳ *Skateboarding in the X-Games*, Christopher Blomquist (PowerKids, 2003)

✳ *The X-Games: Skateboarding's Greatest Event*, Jeff Savage (Capstone, 2005)

Websites

✳ www.exploratium.edu/skateboarding
Find out all about skating and how to do tricks.

✳ www.skateboarding.nu/tricktips/index.html
Find video tips on doing basic moves and stunts.

✳ www.tonyhawk.com
This is Tony Hawk's official website.

If you liked this Atomic book, why don't you try these...?

Index

Notes for adults

Use the following questions to guide children towards identifying features of explanation text:

Can you find the steps needed to complete a tic-tac on page 5?

Can you find an example of a main heading and side heading on page 10?

Can you find two examples of the present tense on page 14?

Can you give examples of connectives from page 22?

Can you give examples of side headings starting with 'how' 'where' and 'what'?